KEN EVANS featured in Broken Sleep's *Masculinity* anthology and won the 2018 Kent and Sussex Poetry Competition. He has been published widely in magazines including *Acumen, Magma, Poetry Scotland, The Alchemy Spoon, Frogmore Papers*. He began to write poetry ten years ago after donating a kidney to his sister who has lupus.

ALSO BY KEN EVANS

POETRY
True Forensics (Eyewear, 2018)
To An Occupier Burning Holes (Salt, 2022)

PAMPHLET
The Opposite of Defeat (Eyewear, 2016)

KEN EVANS
A Full-On Basso Profundo

CROMER

PUBLISHED BY SALT PUBLISHING 2025

2 4 6 8 10 9 7 5 3

Copyright © Ken Evans 2025

Ken Evans has asserted his right under the Copyright, Designs and
Patents Act 1988 to be identified as the author of this work.

*This book is sold subject to the condition that it shall not, by way of
trade or otherwise, be lent, resold, hired out, or otherwise circulated
without the publisher's prior consent in any form of binding or cover
other than that in which it is published and without a similar condition
including this condition being imposed on the subsequent publisher.*

First published in Great Britain in 2025 by
Salt Publishing Ltd
12 Norwich Road, Cromer, NR27 0AX United Kingdom
www.saltpublishing.com

Salt Publishing Limited Reg. No. 5293401

A CIP catalogue record for this book is available from the British Library

ISBN 978 1 78463 335 6 (Paperback edition)

Typeset in Sabon by Salt Publishing

Printed and bound in Great Britain by Clays Ltd, Elcograf S.p.A

For Sheila, George and Harry with all my love

'Gee, but it's hard when one lowers one's guard to the vultures
Now me, I regard it a tortuous hardship that smoulders
Like a peppermint eaten away
Will I fight? Will I swagger or sway?'
STEVE HARLEY AND COCKNEY REBEL,
'Tumbling Down' (1975)

'She just stopped her car on the Heart of America bridge and jumped in the Missouri River, leaving behind a note that said. 'If you get out of life with one friend left, you're probably a kiss-ass.'
RICHARD FORD, 'Be Mine' (2023)

Contents

I: THE OIKOSPHERE — 1
  And the Blithe Shall Eat a Horse — 3
  Bus Replacement Therapy — 4
  The Plaiting of Their Hair — 5
  Purple Iris — 6
  All Our Fathers are a Dark Religion — 8
  The Emotions Macerator Running Vest — 9
  Lucian Freud Drawing His Dead Mother — 10
  To Gasp at the Cold — 12
  The Custom of the Sea — 13
  The Thirst — 14
  The Forgeristas — 15
  Atomic — 16
  The Wolf's Bite — 17
  The Night Before the Op. — 18
  Legit. — 19
  101 Ways to Get Out of Bed (Abridged) — 20
  An Unfamiliar Calling — 21
  AWOL/Gone — 22
  The Optimism Principle — 24
  The Great Escape on the River Leen, Nottingham city centre — 25
  The Wirtschaftswunder (*Economic Miracle*) — 26
  Underneath the Berliner Dom — 27
  White Space for poet Adrian Mitchell (1932–2012) — 28
  A Jab in Bakewell — 29
  Letting Go — 30
  Family Slices — 31
  The Appointment — 32

Climbing the Cage	34
Peeling an Orange by St. Clement's Church	35

II: THE ANERSPHERE — 37

Song of The Wild	39
How the Fritillary Flies	40
An Invisible Fury	41
The Laughter of Mustard and Sea Foam	48
Pineapple Rings and Dostoyevsky	50
No Man's Land	52
Learning the Spit Game in School Break	54
The Distance in a Boy	56

III: AMERICANICITY — 59

Flight Security	61
SpongeBob Lollipops All Over America	62
The Ts & Cs of Private Space Travel	63
Real Diamond Lederhosen	64
The Atacama Oxygen House	65
In a Land of Sleeping Rainbows	66
'Genius at Wrok'	67
A Toughened Glass	68
Ghosts of S. Francisco	69
A Lament for 'My Dear'	71
A Heat Mirage in the Navajo Desert	72
It Don't Mean a Thing (If it Ain't Got that Swing)	73

Acknowledgements — 75

A Full-On Basso Profundo

I: The Oikosphere

'Oikos' – family, household (Greek)

And the Blithe Shall Eat a Horse
after 'Migration' by Karen Solie

Polynesian seafarers navigate by the sway
and bob of their testicles, sitting cross-legged
on the bottom of vegetable-matter boats.
They note the ratio of pitch to roll in the current,
and stay on course by keeping the ratio constant,
believing the ocean moves through them, not they,
through the surf. We won't mute a parking sensor
on our bumper with a wide berth to reverse into.
They sail a quarter of Earth's surface.

At J's Zoom wedding, no-one can tell Aunt E.
her audio isn't live, and her hours of make-up
are frozen on video under her mauve fascinator.
Outside, April's drought goes unnoticed as crisis
overshadows the actual crisis. Dictators loop-
the-loop. People soon talk loud on phones again.
A Little Eaton man spots the Loch Ness Monster.
In a way, he's not far wrong. Rioter's dogs join in
for the free adrenaline, and not their usual walk.

Swallows shut down half their brain to fly, asleep.
I feel we tried this once or twice but couldn't keep
up with the insight, or the trembling flows of data.
The crisis before this, swings back our way again.
I'd like to tell Aunt E., who can't hear, 'I'm fine,
considering.' Stress-induced cortisol in our brain,
shuts down all those functions that get in the way
of survival, like digestion or reproduction. No,
I don't understand it either, Aunty.

Bus Replacement Therapy

again. We sigh and sag under our luggage,
a weekend shot down by a trial of strength,
replacement bus to a replacement train,
no reservations, everyone for themselves,
no-one sat in the First Class plush through
the frosted glass, separating us.

I find a place in Second. A Greek guy enters
through the gasping doors and asks, is that
First Class, where the divide is? I'm unsure
it matters. He says wild, and takes his seat
beyond the glass. Join me, he shouts,
the widest grin in the sweet shop. I'm OK

I say. He stows a bag up top, falls to the plump
seat like it's the last waltzer on the final ride,
turns and says, the legroom, man! I smile,
attend to my shy Kindle. Actual onward travel
later, and the trolley guy halts in the aisle, says
will you have a beer from the gentleman in First

with his compliments? I think of refusing to be
a prefect as no-one should have sway over another.
Spotty pieties. Conviction now in a bot-voice
assures us of the next stop, and what comes after,
Welwyn Garden City, Letchworth, Bedford:
as if we're all good or getting there.

The Plaiting of Their Hair

Readying for societal breakdown, I buy a Makita
Electrosierra, so wild and techy a term, in Spanish:

a 350 mm. blade, UC3-40 chainsaw. 'Work within
shouting distance of someone,' warns the manual.

I fear what I'll find inside the box. '*Sujeter
la electrosierra firmenente con los manos*'.

What if I love the unpacked, the one who chases
the bad guys from our house when they barge in,

fresh from food riots, clutching fat breadknives,
their faces dropping on sight of ear-mufflers, gloves,

wearing what I keep in an outhouse by the woodpile,
biceps the kids can't circumference with their fingers,

the one who, hungry, will kill and keen for when the sun
wasn't so hot and Vikings didn't bear arms by the river.

Uncalloused hands beneath the bathwater, before I share
a bedtime story. I write only my name in this poem, over

and over, but I know that to fell logs is easier than
plaiting hair. Come, I'll show you what I mean, I say.

'*Sujeter la electrosierra firmenente con los manos*' – 'Hold the chainsaw
firmly with two hands.' (Spanish)

Purple Iris

I think you would be clever round your matches
   on dating apps, knowing they are flammable,
and squeeze one before trying, like a satsuma.

I think you would be tall and long-limbed,
   like your swimming brothers who followed,
a bit sporty and awkward maybe, in your teens.

I think, at twenty-four next birthday – what a time
   for you – you'd be doing OK in an alright job,
and as all us ingrates, moan about public transport,

make plans for a ridiculous future. I think, waking
at four, you'd find me guilty-as-charged downstairs,
   and we'd share the one light from a fridge-door

over milk and cereal, and I will try and pull you close,
   ask where you've been all these nights,
scaring us: about as useful as asking why light shines

on one bit of pavement every morning at 11 o'clock
   and why not on the purple iris to the side
who stays courteous but unhappy in the shade.

   Angles and refraction and accident and physics
     explain this life even as they swallow it whole.
       All I know is no-one ever fell out

of a tree without breaking something soft.
    It's enough, except reality goes on
and on and the fall from the high bough snags

leaves, twigs and upturned birds' nest in my hair,
as well as blue pockets of sky to help with what's
    uncopable, the illusion of any 'up'.

I know for all this, thought's a realm of stone, a cairn
    I add a pebble to each year, building a taller tower
to view out from, while shadows grow on a tiny window

of shaded glass, the chapel of rest where I held you
    ten minutes without the midwife,
        putting off letting you go.

All Our Fathers are a Dark Religion

A fish, through the joke
spectacles of the ocean,
sees an H-bomb flash
from thirty miles away,
their scales facing the light
stripped, as with a salty stare
they see us for what we are,
monitor lizards slapping
at sand with tails to flatten
shirred edges, scratching
to un-ink the blind tattoo,
free the itching blood from
a genealogy of self-harm.

We cut and rub the burn
they gifted us, cave paint
for our forearms, a grave
wider than the arc of our
swinging tails that can't
flick both sides at once,
and so well dug, we fall in,
half-agreeably, a not-quite
stumble. His deliberate
mishearing of pop lyrics
was good, too: 'We can be
herons, just for one day.'

The Emotions Macerator Running Vest

My older sister lords it at tea and I'm anxious for what,
if you can actually believe this family, doesn't exist,
erasure even of the erasure, ghosts made of curiosity.

'Are you wearing training bras now?' The straps over
her crew neck. I want to provoke as a brother yet show
the table how grown-up I am with this info., fly all

my flags of confusion, with no knowledge of language
as masculine, and in a tense of the oppressive continuous.
I'm ten, a pea on my fork, in after her to morning blood

in our toilet. She death-ray stares me. Mum is a deflector
shield of silver alloys. In his emotions macerator running
vest, Dad is whizzed, hesitant, equivocal. My sister's fork

drops, pinging peas onto the patio that stick in the pool
filter, threshing our holiday water. Dad stares at his plate
as if crashed somewhere alien, his wound bloodying a salad

he's unsure if to pick from the owner's garden, but picks,
anyway. The umbilical cord pulls my puppy-fat spacesuit
to the capsule. I howl 'Let me go!' And for fifteen seconds,

before the vacuum of space boils, then freezes me to a husk,
I dream. At altitude, the curve of the Earth is a blue decal
stuck to my visor, spinning out on a kiss curl of the sun.

Lucian Freud Drawing His Dead Mother

The artist drew his mother 1,000 times in his studio and
for an hour in the hospital morgue after she died.

She has no need of headgear for open country
for what can burn her forehead now? He draws

no wig, mascara, to mislead death, make it look
elsewhere and pick-on someone other, her mouth

a storm-drain through which all her flesh is sucked.
No lapis beads on her wattled throat, no jewels,

for this is merely death, walked-in from the desert
with sand in every pore of a lumpen uniform.

No background, for what is death's back story, that
it means no harm, is only trying to tidy things and clean?

Nothing says death like the head as a mask, stoppered
at the neck. No need to sketch the muscles of her arms,

for she can no longer pat his own and ask, 'how's it
going, Lucian, dear, may I peek? I'm getting so tired'.

If there's gold on her fingers, it finds no favour
with his quick wrist. The face is all, the sanctuary

of ruin. Black nostrils, empty snail shells. Blood
pools below her skin. He crosshatches, a single

piece of charcoal, the dark torch to spray light,
pressing a cheek from the paper, a hill of bone,

no life here, only his pumping heart misting
in a blue chamber, forcing himself to draw,

motionless on the hard metal fact of his chair,
a celebration of the fought over, each knuckle

on his drawing-hand white and swift and fierce,
like pinned hats at a funeral, over bared necks.

To Gasp at the Cold

Crocs, easier to slip on with my flat arches,
to sneers of being 'Old Bloke's Slippers',
worn in a damp November to pick late
raspberries from drooping canes, to make
our muesli more relevant. Brown leaves in
chilled fingers, I fail to notice one shoe slip-off,
before I put a sock-foot down, not feeling cold
at first, but warm to my unsuspecting reptile
brain, till it seeps through to the ankle bone
and time's big swamp bubbles burst forth into
another time when he was younger,
my hand on his tummy, asking –

does it hurt where dinner lives,
or where your pudding goes? A gravel shore
to dip my toe and hold his hand, to shocked
recoil at the bitter cold, though some urge too,
to wade in deeper, and to remind him
of how he leapt in the Arctic Ocean
on the Lyngen peninsula, north of Tromsø,
and stayed in a whole minute, fifty seconds
longer than the nobodies there, to slide out,
slick as bladderwrack, but for the boreal sand
in his hair, from where he'd touched polar
night, at the bottom.

The Custom of the Sea

Up to the 1880s, cannibalism was entered into at sea. The expression for this act of desperate survival was 'the custom of the sea.'

A cabin boy against three toughened sailors. He gives way to the bosun, who has him tight, lets him cry on his chest, hollowed-out by two weeks hunger. The bosun says, blessings, laddie.

The bosuns' tears fall on his head, as he leans in at the big man's throat, under a sheltering arm that doesn't hold the knife. Say your prayers, laddie, the Lord loves a pious boy.

The heartbeat in the boy rattles the jaw, making teeth chatter. He squints up into sainthood, a sacrifice of the young and tender, the sun on the waves, plumes of white doves, against an ocean's scrim.

The bosun says a psalm as the blade sweeps the neck. Their chronometer box catches the blood so they can drink it warm, imagine it other. Going down, the sun soaks-up the ocean into darkness like an emitted gas.

The heart and liver carved first, through an iron intuition of what is good. They tear bits off the arm above the torn sleeve, where the skin's flayed less red by sun and water.

They grow a different shape, shadows twist behind their ribs, as if knelt for a communion and the slim wafer has burnt a hole in their tongues. A rescuing captain, seeing their brandedness, says nothing.

The Thirst

(i.m. SC)

'I was found by the landlord,' are not words
we'd all wish for as epitaph, but I hear his
laughter, in the gorge of his sickness

saying, 'Why not?' If not found by a lover,
his ex-, or the friend who charges his glass
as they sway by his elbow, then by

whom? Why not the landlord in the room over
the pub, his shortest, most familiar address
of strewn sheets, the pile due for the launderette?

The landlord knocks with a spare, opens up,
says, 'Sorry' loudly, and finds the mauve
lips that breathed rhythm & blues on tenor sax

all the years I knew him, songs of love and loss,
of open roads and neon-lit diners on
sandy highways in the shadow of The Bomb,

without ever leaving South London. You'd not
eaten, the coroner said. A blue amber of compulsion
your diet, lunchtime drinks turning into evenings,

you, on an imaginary Triumph Bonneville, drawing
a full house at The Cartoon pub, in the spot, puckering
down on an upturned flower, lifted to the light.

The Forgeristas

*Once the Locarno Ballroom and later, the new Coventry
Library, The Stranglers play Tiffany's nightclub in 1977*

We stink of bad teachers, piss and hormone-splatter,
and an already sweet remorse for this night having to end.

No mosh or slam pit then, only pogoing. We lose a Doc Marten,
front braces from our teeth, pills and sulphate to slip the pain,

kinetic, naked: a Futurist manifesto caught in a gun barrage.
We chuck raw eggs, gob. They exit, won't don't play for morons

who waste good food when people go hungry. We cheer, anointed
by our heroes as fools. We are missiles hurled at a sacerdotal stage.

They're back for, *whatever happened to Leon Trotsky? He got an ice
pick that made his ears burn. Whatever happened to all*

the heroes, all the Shakespeare-os? The icons we smash-up for parts,
plundering from an old ballroom the crinkling of woven taffeta skirts,

a blue static shooting up a partner's arm, a trouser creased in readiness,
as dancers' spin by dusty books in aisles of library hush, egg yolk

sliding down the faded lettering upon the spines. Hugh Cornwell,
on bass, sees Beckett bouncing through the head mist of a crowd.

Atomic

Schrodinger and Einstein thought quantum entanglement occurs when two particles interact, or share space, such that the quantum state of each can't be described independently, even when separated in space.

Love is science! If we say, 'We are meant
for each other' or 'Even apart, we sense
our togetherness', we re-enact quantum
entanglement, where one particle in a tangled
pair depends on aspects of the other, even if
the duo are light years apart, and whatever's
the space between them.

'We've never been as happy as this,' we claim,
as if the time before our meeting was one long
day of waiting, but weren't we happy once
as kids, with our feet dangled in Llyn Llydaw,
or as students in the Karwendel mountains,
at an almen, unmarked on our map, selling
peaks of frothy, cold beer?

A waiter said pay the cash when next this way,
laughing at the improbability of it. Love's
with us always, even if wearing a cheap suit,
and leaning, a little too composed, on a far,
peeling wall of the universe, refusing a dance.
All we need do is cha cha cha his way across
the floor, fingers entwined, to return to what
we already know, at the sub-atomic level.

The Wolf's Bite

*Lupus is a chronic immune system illness,
and 90% of sufferers are women.*

A fear-frost freezes my mum's face
as she points to the phone, mimes,
'It's important', a finger twisted
in the soft innards of their call,
'it's your sister', as if down the line,
she shouldn't hear me as they share
the news you only want to say once
to your mother:

it's incurable   mostly women
from minorities   not terminal
there are drugs   and in time   dialysis
it's named for an animal's bite   lupus.
In Norse myth, the giant wolf, Fenrir,
bound in chains made by the sound
of cat's footsteps and the breath of a fish,
steals in, to wreak his vengeance

                and so the pack circles
in the dark beyond the TV, voices in
the hall crevassed by silence, a swishing
of legs through a deep fall, a forest of ears,
tundra-hungry teeth. I turn the sound up,
the conversation in the wall, is a vertigo.
The pack-leader, up to his grey haunches,
sniffs the air in billows, sinks his claws
beneath the hard crust of snow.

The Night Before the Op.

A bed at Travelodge, near Hammersmith

hospital, the M4 running up a heatwave.

A sheet only for cover, diesel-thick air

piles like spindrift at an open window.

A truck judders on its shock-absorbers,

grinds up the gears, throaty coughing.

I want to give in to seven temptations

at once, run across a forecourt in scalding

light, banish the headache crawling

my pillow. An overnight bag, ready,

rumples and shifts, small animal noises

under the zip. If sleep comes, it lets itself

in with its own passkey. I miss it.

Legit.

The kidney donor has a temporary loss of courage

It's OK to say 'No', on the trolley to theatre, the surgeon says
like a hostage negotiator, the breeze between her teeth.
Skip it, no questions asked,
run to a reception ward where they marked the spot over
my left hip with black magic marker as in, '*Legit*.'

Ditch the robe with the side-ties like an apron, pull back on
an unwashed t-shirt of '*Legit*,'
reverse from the hospital car park to an open vein
of motorway, bask in the pointless radio blah-blah
as I drive the flash brick ordinary of the streets, all, '*Legit*.'

Back home for breakfast of,
I'm dreaming – I get it – toast and jam and big mugs
of storm-brewed, Yorkshire tea,
the Velcro torn around my heart, as pink as a first thought –
but then you, sister, lying there,

waiting on your own knife, saying nothing, *Legit*.
'Answer,' the sheet cries, the peaks of her toes sticking up
like ears on a ghost, and will charred toast taste,
the high squeak of a new jam jar lid, sound, ever as good
and Legit. again, if I hear a gulped answer of 'No'.

101 Ways to Get Out of Bed (Abridged)

I). The Fosbury Flop:

Using the headboard and a torsion in your back and hips, you twist, rise
in one coiled move over the bar of the mattress, land on your knees,
waiting for the breath you once had, and on with your stick, for a piss.

II.) The Sloping-Off Lover:

You wake at 3 with a start, for the foetal body you find yourself curled
inside; wriggle out, a chrysalis; push your bum up as light steals down
the curtains, your furtive escape called-out by these throaty bedsprings.

III). The Drunk on the Tube:

You rise as if stones hold you down, and break the surface, heavy
as a waterlogged coat, wonder why you are so sticky and slick,
your seaweed-hair, the doors of the Tube, aquarium glass, closing on you.

There's ninety-eight more ways, at least, to reflect on how to free yourself
from the rack, but tea arrives by blue angel, and a sun raised on possibilities.

An Unfamiliar Calling

*The Chaplaincy Office before the op., Hammersmith
Hospital, Department of Spiritual & Pastoral Care*

'Knock if no-one's here!' says a Blu-Tac'd sign
on the door. No answer. I wonder about the
exclamation mark they end on. Is it a wail
or jocose, as if God has wearied of His load
today and they're filling-in, as best they can.
I'm only here as the Multi-Faith Centre's lost
in the labyrinth of ward white and I need a place,
fast, to let the blood calm between my ears now
I know the op. is on for Monday, but this room
isn't quiet, there's a tick-tick of pipes warming,
sending dust spirals to stained glass, and a woman
in the pew behind, who I swear could pray
in a cattle stampede, all her faith in soft hooves,
and me, trying not to sneeze, caught in the silence
only two stilled strangers make when thrown
together by an unfamiliar calling.

AWOL/Gone

Father/Son: like missions over enemy territory –
    radio-silence   coded alarms,
  his medal from Malaya to my ear
    a purple ribbon of screams,
  kampongs ablaze in bamboo fires.
Father/Mother: she sorts his uniforms at 3am.
He jangles less and less on the wardrobe rail
with each jacket of his set aside for charity.

Father/Wing Commander: a listening bunker
    at Kolsas HQ, Oslo, for AFNE/
    Allied Forces Northern Europe.
    The Soviet's an hour away by ICBM/
    Inter-Continental Ballistic Missile.
    I knew my SAMs from my MIGs
      a Mirage from a Phantom,
raised on an Observer's Book of Aircraft (1969).

He should've named me Roger, 'Roger and Out'
    maybe we'd have chatted more.
Son/Father/in pallor-mortis: why not, Dad,
    give me a two-minute warning
    to streak from my bunker to yours
    storm the airstrip   scatter words
like machine-gun fire   before your take-off
    into the thin air of COPD?

Chronic Obstructive Pulmonary Disease/emphysema,
    by any other name   a gurgle in the throat
      the unspoken   over propellor clatter.
Propaganda/truth lost to NAAFI aisles of plenty.
Mum – her oxygen supply cut – tears booze-flamed
at the funeral   talks of the flyer   her own breath
      and heartbeat   who ran out
    of air   circling our atmosphere.

The Optimism Principle

The gods are no more unwilling
to listen than usual and babies still
get pulled from rubble, sometimes.
The Council will never collect old
mattresses, they recline in lay-bys
like nudes, as ever. My gate-latch
only grinds into the strike if forced,
and I forget our lottery tickets again,
which may have won us a tenner,
but March sun still draws strength
from pale daffodils, and rabbits eat
my lettuces in summers now, as
always, and home remains a flicker
of a kitchen light, radio on, some song.

The Great Escape on the River Leen, Nottingham city centre

The call to the Agency clicks to voicemail,
a left message slips cages of river-tossed
supermarket trolleys, dumped for spirogyra
to wrap around their silver cordons. The grey
fuzz of feathers, a mother, guiding a brood
of pillow-down up the bank, over take-out trays.
A banded demoiselle takes a helicopter view, gap-
finding. Crayfish pink their claws at the metal cage,
blind harpists seeking lost strings, by fingertip.

With black, noise-cancelling headphones for eyes,
the caddis-fly weave silk round sand and leaf nests
to coddle their young on the riverbed, as mayflies
tread in yeasty bins of filtered light below beech
trees on the towpath. An Essex skipper leaps
the wires, Steve McQueen on motorbike wings in
The Great Escape we gave up watching Christmases
ago, streaming still on Netflix, in case we need
escape again, in case there is escape.

The Wirtschaftswunder (*Economic Miracle*)

In the unnoticed uniform of the old
they embrace, silver hair shining
under the tower of light in Berlin
Hauptbahnhof. The dome, a huge
mouth, gapes, a metal brace holding
clean glass teeth. A sense of curtains
drawn before night is properly here.
She shakes away this lonely image
of her flat, checks her watch and says
what they always keep for times like
now, and walks to the down escalator.

First her feet, then shins and thighs,
slide to the cafés below; her arms cut-
off at an elbow, the shoulders appear
to rise to meet their own diminuendo.
Lovely to him still, her chin sinks,
her smile enveloped by silver stairs.
The *Wirtschaftswunder* and unity
with the East, all the lives they've
lived so far, *trotz allem*, are nothing
to this time and light, disappearing
now through the down escalator.

Trotz allem – 'in spite of everything' (German)

Underneath the Berliner Dom

Too tired to pick-up an Order of Service,
we collapse in a pew. At the lectern,
below a rendering of sky under the dome,
a woman translates the German of the man,
English as clear as the psalms, unbrokered
by a PA, rising-up the nave to hushed air.

'Forgive us our arrogance.' Not trespasses,
only plain words spoken here. Woman/man,
dual-vocabularies, pews made not for ease,
but to stiffen backbones, this house of faith
over the scorched precinct of a tyrant, words
ringing true as if heard for the very first time.
An arm in hers as organ flutes lift copper light
to warm the red tips of our ears that flame.

White Space for poet Adrian Mitchell (1932–2012)

I sent poems, hubris-mail, with an SAE, to Adrian in 1985,
the envelope sealed and kissed once lightly, for luck,
c/o Alison & Busby, Noel Street, London W1F.
'When you write, find out more about other people,' he replied,
with 'a tenderness found between animals,'
on a red-ribbon typewriter, ever the radical,
and a pen and ink drawing of a smiling elephant
I analysed to death as a student, blowing hazy smoke
off a hangover.
What kindness to not be a director of demolition when he can
take a wrecking-ball at any time to my paper-thin pretensions!
In Ralph Steadman's drawings filling the half-blank spreads
of his *Collected*, there's a similar white space
for discretion, while abjuring nothing,
a wimple worn over the crown,
framing his forehead, pale as my title page.

John Berger said of Adrian Mitchell: 'Against the present British state
he opposes a kind of revolutionary populism, bawdiness, wit, and the
tenderness sometimes to be found between animals.'

A Jab in Bakewell

He leads her to the chair,
leans the stick against a wall,
her hair the colour of vapour
trails from a space capsule
re-entering. They are the ten-
fifteen. A woman says she's ten-
twenty. I'm twenty-five past,
early for my own puncturing
of anxiety.

He lets go, elbows crooked
and ready in case she sways,
against a pharmacy shelf.
'Where are you?' she calls.
'Here', he says. 'beside you'.
'I know, but I can't see you.'
He returns to her, his belt hangs
loose, missing the last loop at his
trouser waist. She hangs on to it,

peers round, as if the room is candle-lit
and receding. 'Don't pull,' he says,
'or my trousers'll fall down,' just a bit
rehearsed, this joke for us, waiting.
He holds her hand as he reads for her
and she biros the consent form.
'It says here, Mum, are you pregnant?'
'I don't think so,' she replies, lucid
as Derbyshire weather.

Letting Go

I steer Beth out in her covered poem,
one wheel wobbly and a faulty brake lock,
heap clothes on her for all I know of wind,
rain, ink and travel, and wrap the soft lines
of crocheted woollens round her.

She talks to herself like a churned river,
shakes a small fist at shopfronts and cars,
for my singular, rapt attention. She cries
me to a fitful sleep or will turn me over,
waking from my dream, to smile.

She knows well aren't I the lucky man.
I drop her off, leave her to all she must
see for herself through
those long dark eyelashes I kiss.

Family Slices

It's only pizza, mother. We're sat with those
we trust, and only slightly resent, for showing
such faith. On portions, she grows vague.

We can order one each, or a big one to share.
Mum is like she never heard of such a thing.
My wife volunteers to slice hers for her.

She acts as if she's never seen a pizza cutter
wheel – what frivol! No-one not strong
stomached enough should eat with us.

I try and arrange the conversation like flowers,
the stalks in sugar water, the blooms out front.
She takes on the acquired helplessness of age.

She wants less of what anyone else is having.
Our son's girlfriend distracts her other ear,
helping calm Mum's feelings of exposure.

I make a forkful of basil and mozzarella, feed
her slowly from the tines, sip white wine spritzer,
my wife a watchful ripple in the tilting yellow.

Someone not me, but who looks a lot like, calls
for more pizza. Mum chews the sourdough, bites
her lip in disapproval, or in fear of disapproval.

The Appointment

I take the road I don't drive now,
to not my usual surgery,
a route undriven since the kids
were little, in booster seats,
with child-locks. This stretch
we wild-camped once,
now a new Aldi supermarket.

There's actual tarmac for trucks
to rattle the glazing in windows
of the new estate. An ironmongers
becomes a betting-shop. Other
young dads drive their kids out
for fresh air and bonding, hilly walks.
Their kids grumble like ours, once.

The astronaut on Radio 4 says
space shouldn't be so strange to us,
it's only a hundred kilometres over
our heads, the distance equivalent
of Sheffield to Manchester, via the A57
Snake Pass, and thinning like on Venus
to clouds of sulphuric acid,

I turn onto the road I skidded on
way back when, hitting a tractor,
to spin in a planetary slow swerve
of a world starring into constellations

in my crazed windscreen. Nobody
was in the backseat then, thank god,
and this heart beating faster than the doc

says, today, is really advisable. The very
same lay-by where I stopped to catch
my breath, and wind down a window.
Now, driver-side glass drops in a press
of a button. I remember a chrome handle,
the air winched-down to greet me.

Climbing the Cage

We climb the wire, one leg over
the flash of a 'Hazard' sign, steal
nothing but warnings: 'If the police
catch you, don't call us up.'

Portakabin prised with a spanner.
The scatter of drill-bits by the on-
switch, squeals of laughter, dust
shimmers, a vibrating handle,

tickling in our small grip. A menace
of hot metal. Fingers into overalls
on hooks, for fags, pics, coins,
the no-point clutter of grown-ups.

We're natives to skimmed surfaces,
play footie with rolls of gaffer tape,
toolbox for posts, pee on the fresh
plaster, leave our wall shadow stink.

Peeling an Orange by St. Clement's Church

What might three hundred and fifty years
      of undertaking do
to one family's DNA? Are tact and discretion
      bred into the genome?
      The fierce innocence of knowing
and forgiving all our blemishes and stop-holes?

A trade passed through clean half-moon
    fingernails to offspring, their offspring
    and so on, the latest generation all over
the new trend for QR codes on gravestones.
    Today's overseer in a black mullet
    with an unjacketed, tartan waistcoat.

The bench by the church remembers Betty,
who liked it here says a plaque, as do we, sat
    peeling oranges in the sun. The skins curl,
    blanched like beach plastic on the seat arm.
We sip well-water with a metal of the anchor on
which Clement was tied, swimming to sainthood.

Sink or swim, is the teak exterior and gold handle
of mariners. I doff a baseball cap with sticky fingers,
    as the hearse pulls up, opposite.
The coffin bounces in the ruts, till the strong arms
    of the business lift it out to raise it skyward,
    and the gathered there, check phones for silent.

II: The Anersphere

(Greek – 'aner' – male).

Song of The Wild

Ukrainian soldiers sent to the front are offered a visit to a sperm bank

A
dandelion seed
flying into sun
the flickering sub-title
to all the world's languages
specks on shaky old film
one lucky one clings to an egg wall
the prize almost nothing
while being it all –
'the ability to make sperm
evolved only once
600 million years ago' –
is what it's all about
it's all about what is
what it's all about is
endless variation
bountiful buddhahood
same and different
under one franchise
a bear at an ant hill swats tiny red feet
huge paws can't hold   an ice-pool plunger
slaps blood back into sunburned shoulders
yelping in an ant-frenzy of red eyelid
nobody dictates this
it's merely summer in paradise
crammed into one afternoon
releasing back to the wild
the impossible urge
to live

How the Fritillary Flies

A caterpillar spits a sac of silk and if
each cell contains the entire sequence
of who or what a creature is,
how is it one clump of cells knows to
line up, side by side, and turn into wings,
then shut-off? While another clump blinks
on spilling pigment to the creature's
green blood, waves of colour flowing
into the wing scales, glossy gloves
that slide in pockets on the wings,
brown, black, orange, silvery-white, each zone
only receptive to the one colour it's destined
to become, to let wings unfold, wet from
making, and for a dangerous moment,
hold steady, to dry the double-layer,
one side loud to ward off foes, the other,
a lure to mates, as pattern-making
cells go dormant for the butterfly to
master flight, amazing us,
and not suggesting a ship's bell,
swaying in the swell before a storm.

An Invisible Fury

*In northern England, a 100+ km. of cave passage is
yet to be discovered, including entire cave systems
(The Council of Northern Caving Clubs)*

THE ACTION:

Boom-boom go the bridges at Matlock,
the Square & Compass, Grouse & Claret, a humpback
at Baslow, the one-way crossing with lights at Chatsworth.

※

It's Sunday and the world sleeps. Five stone bridges,
blown apart by a recipe from Asda,
Aldi, the agri-wholesaler at Darley Dale.

※

One blast every ten minutes from 3am,
no-one dies, but in super-sizing terror, terror is
the imagination of terror, our fear of what's to come.

※

In the National Park, there's been no cool summers
since 1996. We don't remember
or cancel this.

The bombs rip Derbyshire along the Derwent River,
the gorge at High Tor, Matlock Bath, a deeper gash now
in the minds of locals. Security services look baffled.

Who does this to rain-streaked, millstone farms
squared-off like graph paper by dry-stone walling?
Our media has tales of barbarians at motorway slip-roads.

The brass band in Youlgreave by Lathkill Dale,
named 'Pommies'*, from when all they knew to play was
Pom-Pom-Pom, draw a fresh breath between their lips.

THE ACTOR:

Rachel is rid of male *Sieg Heils* and their New Balance trainers,
her new home a cave and her mortgage, the climate. Mao, the killer
of a billion sparrows in the Great Leap Forward*, is small fry.

She knows her Shelley (the other one)* and that Frankenstein
said Peak caves are 'cabinets of natural history',
where heat-seeking probes can't see, and drones fall like Icarus.

Our moon so much better known than these, and a cave a relief
from heat, a camp-bed and a stove under poisoned pastures.
MI5 tells farmers, be ready for food insecurity by '29.

Food riots seem a stretch in a place Byron dubbed 'Little
Switzerland,'* and the entrance to her lair, hidden by hives,
a placid front-of-house in limestone hills, once coral beds.

In her own changing, she/they, sees the oil barons grow
eight pairs of buttocks and shit black shit
copiously out from each, upon our earth.

Of the Order of Druids and a man of the cloth,
Thomas Eyre, carved thrones and altars on Rowtor Rocks*,
drew serpent and chalice side by side on village outcrops.

A plurality unshared by those with no such ambivalence,
who drag family comfort from priest holes at Hathersage,
for disembowelment before a crowd in Derby*.

REACTION:

A quarry siren, more stone blasted for motorways.
They bomb the gash in the ground, though who in proper mind,
destroys the already demolished? Their point, exactly.

'If your enemy is temperamental, seek to irritate him'*.
They's voice, two octaves lower and with hirsute chest,
holds a mirror to oil-cult brethren, their dying apocrypha.

❦

The year we lose is 2030, when caves miss pipistrelles,
whole species fall to parched peat, on Kinder Edge,
our times like the boiled Permian, a million years since.

❦

Birds cast to metaphor, but Youl-grave or -greave,
'Giolgrove'* in Doomsday, a changeling place, Highways and
Ordnance Survey can't agree their name-calling.

❦

Here, cave-black bees with sunlight shot through
their hoops, guard a queen, and millstone grit and limestone
meet, as radon floats in the gap between hard and soft terrain.

❦

These caves, a shadow-face of the shining moon, alter ego
of tundra and rainforest, spark new grief for places
we never knew and surely now, never will.

❦

In Bradford Dale where sheep 'wool like foam,' washed,
say the words on stones*, the whole stream
a cascade of bleating, now lost, to a dull brown smudge.

THERE'S NO POSTSCRIPT TO APOCALYPSE:

Renewing the rage in 2032, she/they earns the title
of an 'Invisible Fury', as elusive
as swifts that no-one sees coming or know still exist.

The wallabies of Riber Zoo, escaping Matlock's castle folly*,
the zebras and the black cats, all more sightings
than of the 'Fury', in their mole-lit burrow.

Testosterone patches like Nicorettes enlarge their sex,
a wind-turbine engorges on a hilly horizon,
white arms semaphoring, 'Save Our Souls'.

Their chest widens, body fat visits as an unlikely guest.
Their menstruating is a lost history like Dale's miners
selling lead for shot to Cromwell, to win a Civil War.

The young fight the old, winning lawsuits
against informed dinosaurs who knew the score, and still
robbed children of their seasons.

Reparation swag though, won't hold bloated rivers long,
There's no recourse for Atlantic storms,
Thames Barrier overwhelmed, Hull, Liverpool, underwater.

A panto cow at Youlgrave Hall, Carbon face and Methane arse,
moos, 'Show us the science!' They, now full-on basso profundo
bellow, 'Behind you, it's behind you! Close the spigot off, now!'

Notes:

1. In 1860, when the villagers of Youlgrave, Derbyshire, first had musical instruments, all they could play was 'Pom-Pom-Pom.' The villagers became known as 'Pommies.'

2. In China, in 'The Great Leap Forward'(1958-62), Chairman Mao ordered the killing of house sparrows as 'vermin'.

3. Mary Shelley wrote 'Frankenstein' in 1818.

4. Romantic poet Lord Byron (1788-1824) dubbed Matlock Bath in the Derbyshire Peak District as 'Little Switzerland'.

5. The Reverend Thomas Eyre, an 18th century pastor in Birchover, also celebrated as a Druid, carving pagan symbols and thrones on Rowtor Rocks by the village. Some said to inspire local tourism, others claim for rituals held there.

6. In 1588, Padley Hall, Thomas Eyre's family home, was raided and two Jesuit priests were found in hiding. Nicholas Garlick and Robert Ludlam, both local men, were taken to Derby where they were hung, drawn and quartered.

7. Sun Tzu was a Chinese military general and philosopher, who lived sometime between 771 and 256 BC.

8. 'Youlgreave' is the most misspelt village in Derbyshire. The Council road sign on entering the village uses the spelling 'Youlgreave', although the Highways Agency use 'Youlgrave'. Ordnance Survey maps use 'Youlgreave'. Locals use 'Youlgrave.'

9. Words from stones carved on a wall by a pool in Bradford Dale, Derbyshire, where farmers used to take sheep to wash.

10. The folly of Riber Castle, near Matlock, was used as a wildlife park from the 1960s until 2000. When it closed, exotic animals were rumoured to have escaped and their descendants said to live out in secret on the moors.

The Laughter of Mustard and Sea Foam

We're not bedside vigil
or drawn ward curtains,
forced banter or hushed
voices on a waterbed

of solace. We won't
discuss the death
of elephants as a proxy
for the loss

of our neurodivergent
from societal shaming.
We're not backslapper
blokey, we don't reek

of bonhomie. We grind
our words like pebbles,
rolled round the mouth,
taste the grit in our spittle.

You went to save a party
once, at the late-night store,
but didn't read a label
properly and hauled home

32 cans of 0% alcohol.
You hated to be laughed at.
You spun a girl around
the red wine room on huge

grey shoulders for the whole
of Heaven 17's 'Temptation',
4 minutes 37 seconds in
the 12-inch version.

I grab this moment to say
your yellow coat for safari
may upset the elephants,
who mistake you for a banana.

'I's not yellow', you say,
'I's mustard and seafoam.'
Which cracks us up.

Pineapple Rings and Dostoyevsky

the young, wannabe writer,
pale, a deep sleeper,
with a morbid fear of being
thought dead as he dozes,
writes a precocious note
for a bedside table saying
should you find me like this don't
bury me for five days, better safe

than sorry. This comes back
on the day of his fake execution.
waiting his turn with a firing-squad,
facing a pre-dug grave,
he swears if there's a way to gain
a day – a red sun, this mist afloat
over pinking, Petersburg cobbles,
he will write, 'the sunlight is lovely.'

Two men walk away from the chippy,
and weather and sport, the latest slew
of political travesty,
won't do for chatter today.
Evasion, banter, bluster,
can't disguise the anguish
in the shaking trees, walking
the winding path home.

One man stops, says to the trees,
'It's my heart, mate.' Some men
bare their nipples to the moon at such

news, go grease their face and howl,
and if straight-nosed Romans on passing
titter at their simple costume and gaudy
woad, so what? But 'are you done with
them?' is all the other one says, an eyebrow
raised to the crying man's pineapple rings
in their batter, sticky and salty and sweet.

No Man's Land

The car rises on hydraulic legs. He steps
under to tut and blow his cheeks out,
shake a head and rub rust between his
fingers, listing out loud what's wrong:

Rocker arm, gudgeon pin, worn chain,
suspension, driveshaft, timer, shocks
and piston rings. He tells me what he
can and cannot bodge. I avoid his eye.

A name on a wall in the grime. 'Is that
your grandad?' 'Tha's him, alright.
Charabancs for rent for scenic tours.
'E lost it all, requisitioned in't war.'

'Great War? Was he at Polygon Wood
like others round here?' He looks at me
as if it's a test. 'Was 'e 'eck! Never left
'is home, and 'e made 'a killing on it,

it paid for this, the compensation from
the Ministry.' He surveys the garage,
the bumperless panels of sightless cars
at high points in their decomposition,

'an' still he left me Dad in debt.'
In gloom I stare across No Man's Land,
an empty sky, without binoculars, before
he takes pity and makes his bid.

Our chat screws down the spiral
thread it always takes. 'You want to count
the damage, while I wait?' I overstep
the mark. He shrugs, no odds to him.

He draws his baccy pouch from a pocket.
Rolls one. 'It'll cost?' Money,
a secret shame we share. 'I don't 'Swipe'.
You can backdate a cheque. I trust you.

Learning the Spit Game in School Break

take
a slippery
drool
slide it
from
your lower
lip
let it
dribble
a slow
gob
not snap-
ping mid-
plunge
until
the last second
then draw
a finger
through
the gloop
a spit-rope
till you –
a killer
of the mucosal –
sever it before
it splashes
to the ground.
The one who
slices it
nearest

the floor
without it
touching earth
is the winner.
No glassy
jellyfish
gel must fall
on
the thin
dirty shoulders
of your leather
school shoe.

The Distance in a Boy

'I can do my own hair
in the bath.' She's pleased
I'm slowly growing up,
and smiles for my lie.

It takes an age to ease
the shirt over my gashed
back, stuck dried
with blood. I lower

into hot water behind
a locked door, gasp
to take in breath,
giddy

for blood swirled down
the plug, a scrawled
signature I can't see
in a bathroom mirror.

I stow the shirt
out of sight, let
the blood dry a same
colour as the check.

Next, how to do
a wash without
suspicion falling
on me like a dumbbell?

How to choose right
Setting, time, how
the baffling distance men
need in love, enters a boy.

III: Americanicity

Flight Security

the childish optimism of brands
accessing the dream of an aeroplane.
gels and liquids to fill the pores,
Testers and Tasters of duty-free,
a tallow path to a sunlit heaven.

in flux, steadied by plangent
universals of Abba and Vivaldi,
a womb-beat of announcement,
the broken treaties of take-off
and landing, as air lifts us up

or drags us down. Breaking News
breaking still, half an hour later.
my hip sings out of metal sympathy
at Security, a bat-detector pinking
at my upside-down eyes.

SpongeBob Lollipops All Over America

*i.m, Erin West and Ruby Vergara, Wisconsin
school shooting 16 December 2024*

She processes what's behind her eyes with a SpongeBob lollipop,
SPONGEBOB LIVES AT BIKINI BOTTOM IN A PINEAPPLE,
her lips turning as red as the scream in the teacher's mouth.
SPONGEBOB LIVES WITH HIS FRIEND GARY, A SNAIL,
her blonde, second-grader plaits, curl over her head like a shell.
SPONGEBOB AT WORK AT KRUSTY KRABS' RESTAURANT,
the teacher's leg, all bloody, on the classroom floor,
'DROP AND FLOP LIKE A FISH' SINGS PAINTY THE PIRATE,
she's hungry for lunchbreak, still in English, as shots ring out.
SPONGEBOB FINDS IT HARD TO FOCUS OR CONCENTRATE,
she only takes her lollipop out to speak to the CNN reporter,
EXCEPT WHEN HE BLOWS BUBBLES OR HUNTS JELLYFISH,
a swallow of juice she keeps stoppered in her cheek, to savour,
KRABS, ON SPONGEBOBS'S PATTY, 'SO, I TASTE OF THIS?'
and no-one will prise open the pursed lips to speak till she's ready.
The ninth-grade shooter has thrown lollipops against lockers
and classrooms all over school, strawberry-flavour, sugar-free, red.

The Ts & Cs of Private Space Travel

1. You're 18+, under 100 kilos, a max. of one-ninety centimetres; confident of walking to a Launch Tower (7 flights of stairs) in 90 seconds; you can step over ramps and obstacles; dress yourself in a one-piece zip suit, without the aid of a valet.

2. You are sanguine at the top of a tower, 30 metres up with only a metal rail to hold you; you can fasten and unfasten your harness in 15 seconds, which we liken to buckling a seat belt in unfamiliar, chauffeured cars, in the dark, after cocktails.

3. You can sit strapped in your seat for up to 90 minutes, if there's a launch delay, without access to a lavatory; you are relaxed with 5 other people, with the hatch closed – the capsule – the width of two roulette tables or your walk-in wardrobe.

4. You are comfortable to feel three times your normal weight pushing you into your seat for 2 minutes at lift-off; you can clearly hear our mission control, when the noise-level is 100 decibels, less than the sound system in your Italian palazzo.

5. On descent, you experience five-and-a-half times your body weight push down; you must be able to lower yourself out of the capsule on landing, the same height as dropping to a Keshan carpet from a Barberini & Gunnell dining-table.

Real Diamond Lederhosen

the most expensive, diamond-covered lederhosen, cost £69,000.

To pose in diamond deerskin lederhosen
with hand-buffed fasteners of antler horn
at #Livingmybestlife, is a cry for help,

or missing something. When Oprah coined
the meme, she meant to imply our fullest life
and not mere affluence, and we surely know,

even with the few cards we're dealt and the trumps
we bluff to hold – that all our selfies of a new car,
holiday, haute couture – miss a bigger brag we all

share, including J. of Frankfort, Wisconsin, searching
for an origin story, in gem-encrusted lederhosen by
Lodenfrey of München. Ask a true Bavarian,

everyday lederhosen are to last a lifetime, like our skin,
the body glove we shine in, without exceptionalism,
a cover-all camisole, no stein or red wine can stain.

A sense, lost to Instagram and Pinterest, of comfort
in our real *trachten*, smoothed in all the best places,
and weathered by each breath, in

and out, and softened to memory in the rub of thighs,
the supple give of yielding, candid flesh, as memes
flutter over our good fortunes, so much space debris.

Trachten – traditional Germanic costume

The Atacama Oxygen House

Five thousand metres high, and air's
slow striptease in mountain light finds
my own breath wanting, as if arrived
by wet straw gripped in boxing gloves:
small gasps. A gaucho swallows a first
gulp, whooping for a first full house
at cards after long days on the trail,
her spurs dig in a dirt floor, the window
with the missing pane, taped closed.

The roadside house where night or day,
they take you in and sit you down
to wait your turn at a flaking oxygen
cylinder, as long as the truck made it
over the coughing pass with a fresh
delivery. Urgent hands help twist a tap,
a fistful of blue veins freeing the air
to hiss down the pipe to a plastic mask,
misting and clearing, misting and clear.

In a Land of Sleeping Rainbows

*Outlaw Butch Cassidy, officially shot dead in Bolivia in 1908,
lived out in Utah till he was seventy, three witnesses claim.*

He sits, like any old man with egg from
breakfast down his plaid shirt, and creaks
at the hip when he rises, after years riding
the sticking-out ears of the wind. Flies dry
on the polish as his boots bake out front.
No-one here says what they know:

Butch is reborn. Proof in the Lord, if ever
you needed it, unlike the electric sub-
station State legislature promises each year:
our very own son of perdition, and who in
these hills of two hundred souls, dare be
a 'snitch', when a two-day ride from being

unknown by their Christian name? As sap
from the piñon tree softens our sunburn,
our conscience is eased by a story he never
drew first. Boys *sluffing* school, men who
reach into a cow to calm the beast when
their birthing calf isn't presenting straight,

none have a word to say. Women walk slow
by his place on their way to chapel. Families
gazing at a meteor shower, watch who creep
toward him. Few think what the planet looks
like from others, as the stars tread their mute
footfall, splash a long light on dark doorsteps.

sluffing – 'Skipping' in Utah dialect.

'Genius at Wrok'

says his tee, and on the back,
'*This Aint No Work for the Weak*': his eyebrows snag
cloud at a fridge-door, filling chiller cabinets at the gas station
with Ben & Jerry's   Häagen-Daz   Rocky Roads
three Salted Caramel   a slow week on the Vanilla.
It ain't planting trees or saving drips on irrigation channels
nor fixing solar panels but the checkouts love his upbeat call
of 'Sowhaddyagotguys?' He gets invites to their nuptials
that last like gelato in a power outage   but who's gonna soothe
your burning throat today   the water   solar   or chiller guy?

There's always ice cream when you're melting
in Southern Utah, the mercury gone mental these three weeks
in a row   his mom wheezing like nothing you ever want
to hear. Gas station doors swing behind him like he's a croupier
exiting with the house winnings when he's only making the rent
like the rest of us   boots rubbing in the swelter that enlarges
his feet. He exits shouting its gonna be north of forty next week
but hey at least we're not in El Paso   to which gales of laughter
for that well-known armpit of the world
by Mexico's broiled torso.

A Toughened Glass

Brian Cox, cheeks of English red apples, stares up at stars
on the motel TV with five hundred channels and one, five
thousand miles away, on which he's saying, 'the world is
beautiful to look at, yet more beautiful to understand.'
Dust drifts in from the aircon as I fidget with the buttons,
a sprinkler pimps the lawn so green I thought it Astroturf,
each swivel tightening an unsnappable sky another notch,
as the argon seeps from the window at 1% a year, the seals
cracking on the hot, Byway 12, Garfield County glass.

Ghosts of S. Francisco

six blocks east and the X campus glows
  like orthodox bullion   a four-minute hike
to Uber HQ   ghosts in a doorway wait on
    a blood donation of a dollar.

Middle-age white Caucasian male
    jetlag slipping down his eyelids
            like sweat
                  on a Crimplene shirt

the corner of 8th and Market   two guys shuffle by
  at the lights ˙ fidgety   discuss the virtues
of Whole Foods versus Walmart foil.
   'Walmart rips, man, after one hit'

fentanyl cut with spice and mace.
     Sun   no choice   but to shine
picks out their bare toes   small root
    veg. picked early for earthy sweetness.

'You got shorts or longs,' the one advising
    says to the one advised. Google
    says the man is talking syringes
in a sub-culture   if you don't know you don't

know   a cop car glides by   one finger
  salutes all round   no blue light   not worth
the paperwork   crazies enough down the precinct.
    'Your pants are too tight, man'

yells a woman   he shrinks the English way
   by auto-suggestion   like a rube   a crackle
   and hiss of a language he's not tuned-to
     she throws her top off   whirls

it in the sun   time's a slow crash
  her breasts   wardrobe doors
 opening on a rail of hangers
quivering in a draught.

A Lament for 'My Dear'

*Since the first mobile call in New York in 1973, most
people haven't written a letter in 10 years (CBS News)*

dear mum   dear dad   dear human
dear dog who died   if you are up there
dear Registered Address   will you talk to me
the brown, old-fashioned way?

Dear Mama   2Pac wrote in song
dear God   sang a gospel choir
dear Mama sang Linton Kwesi Johnson
in fearful despair   I hope you get this

and it finds you well   dear darling dear diary
dear Muse   dear all
dear groundless optimism   dear hope
you're good   dear cloud how ya' doin

up there!   Dear John Lennon   imagine!
Dear rumours   I can't take any more
'Right dere and welbeloved' wrote Margaret
of Anjou seven centuries ago to no-one

she'd admit to   starting a craze for love letters
which only in December   only in Finland
do they still get snowed under by   words
for a man in a floppy hat and the lit, red antlers

so dear compassion   dear outrage   dear
I regret to inform you   dear sorry we haven't
been able to contact you   please get back
by return   yours always

A Heat Mirage in the Navajo Desert

> Nobody should be wrong to be
> so beautiful in this world
> *(Self-Portrait as Othello*, J. Allen-Paisant)

Nádleehi live their uncertainty
        happy   uncaring
of a single descriptor   their gaze
knowing change is
always here
    present
self-assured   malleable   insistent
layered

shifting like lichen on a red boulder
morphing to green lizards in a mirage
or a red headed vulture that squats to pee
through the folds of a skirt in the desert
as a woman grinning back at us
in the sparkles of sweat hung from our eyelids
a beaded curtain   the earth transfigured
diamond facets of ochre umber sienna orange.

---

* In Navajo culture, the first gender is women, as it's a matrilineal society; second, men. The third are nádleehí, who are born male but function in the role of a woman. The fourth is also nádleehí, born biologically female but functioning as men.

It Don't Mean a Thing (If it Ain't Got that Swing)

*'Where there is love and inspiration, I don't think
you can go wrong' (Ella Fitzgerald)*

Ella, the Queen, King and Ace of Hearts,
thinking she'll goof it up a few bars, stays for the whole whitewater
raft of the trumpet solo, cascading riffs that cram and twist
their notes round every pearly granite stone
in a foam of sound and motion. The crowd awed at how her boat
beats at the waves, is tossed   *ah-hee-hee-dah*   and man – still floats!
dy-doo-da-doo-da-dey   Ella makes her song-splash in the spotlight,
falling as sweat and blessings, drawn from deep inside,
the best drum-solo you ever heard
from a human throat, followed by a raspy sax,
from somewhere in her larynx
that no-one else could ever swoon out so sweet
Blee-blee-blu   boh-di-boh-di-boo   dohti-di-bap-boo   sh'bam sh'bam

Acknowledgements

A special thank you to Chris Hamilton Emery at Salt, Emma Simon and Adrian Buckner, for their support, example and encouragement.

Fourteen of the poems in this collection, or earlier variants, have appeared in print or been mentioned in recent competitions, including:

'The Optimism Principle', Winner, 'On the Move, poems on buses, Guernsey International Competition 2024.
'The Thirst', *Under the Radar* magazine 34, Autumn 2024.
'The Night before the Op.' – *Lighthouse Literary Journal*, 2024.
'Dostoyevsky and Pineapple Rings' and 'The Laughter of Mustard & Sea Foam' *Masculinity* anthology, Broken Sleep Books, 2024.
'Family Slices', *Live Canon* anthology, 2023.
'Purple Iris', runner-up, Arts University of Bournemouth Competition, 2023.
'Flight Insecurity', Poetry Scotland, 2023.
'The Wolf's Bite', *Acumen* shortlist 2024.
'A Lament for 'My Dear'', a winner, Derby Poetry Festival, 2024.
'The Ghosts of San Francisco', highly commended, Poets & Players, 2023
'Lucien Freud Drawing his Dead Mother', *Alchemy Spoon* magazine, 2024.
'Climbing the Wall', *Ink, Sweat & Tears*, 2023.
'The Forgeristas', Hastings Poetry Competition, 2024.

'To The One with Untimely Reminders of the Perils of Kidney Donation', Video for Wells Festival of Poetry, 2024.

Thank you to these magazines, festivals and competitions – you keep all things going.